A ROOKIE BIOGRAPHY

ROBERTO CLEMENTE

Baseball Superstar

By Carol Greene

CHILDRENS PRESS ®

CHICAGO

This book is for Cliff Mitchell.

Roberto Clemente (1934-1972)

Library of Congress Cataloging-in-Publication Data

Greene, Carol.
    Roberto Clemente : (baseball superstar) / by Carol Greene.
        p.   cm. — (A Rookie biography)
    Summary: Describes the athletic achievements and philanthropic deeds
of the professional baseball player who died in a plane crash in 1972.
    ISBN 0-516-04222-X
    1. Clemente, Roberto, 1934-1972—Juvenile literature. 2. Baseball
players—United States—Biography—Juvenile literature. 3. Pittsburgh
Pirates (Baseball team)—Juvenile literature. [1. Clemente, Roberto, 1934-
1972. 2. Baseball players. 3. Blacks—Biography. 4. Puerto Rico—
Biography.] I. Title. II. Series: Greene, Carol. Rookie biography.
GV865.C45G74   1991
796.357′092—dc20
    [B]   91-12664
                                                         CIP
                                                          AC

Roberto Clemente
was a real person.
He was born in 1934.
He died in 1972.
Clemente was a great
baseball player who cared
about other people.
This is his story.

TABLE OF CONTENTS

Roberto and his mother, Luisa Clemente

Chapter 1

Born to Play

"Roberto was born
to play baseball,"
said his mother,
Luisa Clemente.

Many boys on the island
of Puerto Rico
loved baseball.
But Roberto loved it
so much, he would
rather play than eat.

When he was five,
he threw rubber balls
against the wall
in his room.
He wanted to
practice his catching.

While he listened
to games on the radio,
he squeezed a rubber ball.
He wanted to build up
his throwing arm.

The Clemente family
did not have a lot of money.
They couldn't buy
real baseballs for Roberto.

So he and his friends
made their own balls.
They wrapped string
around old golf balls.
Then they wrapped tape
around the string.

They weren't great baseballs.
But the boys used them
until they fell apart.
Then they made new ones.

Roberto's parents, Melchor and Luisa Clemente

The Clemente family
lived in the town of
Carolina, Puerto Rico.
Roberto's father worked
for a sugarcane company.

Melchor Clemente was
a strict father.
He made his
children work hard.
But they loved him.

Roberto had jobs, too.
Early each morning,
he took milk
to his neighbors.
Then he went to school.

When he got older,
he helped his father
load and unload trucks.

"I want you to be
a good man,"
said his father.
"I want you to work."

So Roberto worked.
But no matter what
he was doing, he kept
thinking about baseball.

At last he was almost
old enough to go
to high school.
The high school had
real baseballs and gloves,
and a playing field, too.

Roberto could hardly wait.

Chapter 2

Getting Started

Before high school,
no one knew how good
Roberto would be at sports.
He was small and shy.
But at high school,
he began to shine.

Clemente hits
a home run
in the 1971
World Series.

He ran like the wind.
He was Most Valuable Player
on the track team.
He could throw a javelin
195 feet and jump
six feet into the air.

Best of all, he played
shortstop on the baseball team
and made the all-star team
three times in a row.

One day, Roberto went
to a nearby town.
He wanted to practice
with the Crabbers.
This team played
winter baseball.

Clemente joined the
Santurce Crabbers,
a winter baseball
team in Puerto Rico.

The players let Roberto play
and the owner watched.
That same day,
he gave Roberto a job.

Then a scout for the
Brooklyn Dodgers came
to Puerto Rico to look
for new young players.

Clemente scores
the winning run
for the Crabbers
in their 1954
championship
game.

Roberto went to the tryouts.
So did 71 others.
The scout watched.
He sent 71 players home.
But he wanted to make
Roberto a Dodger—right then.

Mr. Clemente said Roberto
must finish school first.
Then, in the spring of 1954,
Roberto signed a contract
with the Dodgers.

He left sunny Puerto Rico
for Montreal, Canada.
The Dodgers had
a farm team there.

Everything looked good
for Roberto Clemente.
But that year in Canada
turned out to be a
hard year after all.

The Dodgers weren't ready
for him to come to Brooklyn.
But they didn't want
other teams to see
what a good player
Roberto was.

So when he played well,
the manager of the farm team
took him out of games.
Roberto didn't understand.
He felt hurt and angry.

Roberto spoke Spanish.
The other players on his
team spoke English.
People in Montreal spoke French.
He couldn't talk to anyone.
So Roberto felt lonely, too.

Sometimes he thought
he should give up and
go back to Puerto Rico.
But then something happened
—something wonderful.

Clemente with his 1956 Pirate outfield teammates (above, left
to right) Frank Thomas, Lee Walls, Bill Virnon, and with Cuban
pitcher Gonzalo Naranjo (below)

Chapter 3

The Young Pirate

The Dodgers were trying
to hide Roberto
on their farm team
in Montreal.
But scouts from Pittsburgh
saw him anyway.

"We'll take him," they said,
and Roberto Clemente
began to play right field
for the Pittsburgh Pirates.

Clemente leaps to catch a long fly ball.

The fans loved him.
He could leap, catch the ball,
and throw it while
he was still in the air.
He batted well, too.

Clemente crosses the plate after getting his 2,000th hit in 1966.

Even pain couldn't stop
Roberto from playing then.
He had hurt his back when
a drunk driver hit his car.
Roberto played anyway.

But the young Pirate had
one problem—his temper.

Once, he got so mad that
he broke 22 helmets.
He had to pay a big fine.
After that, Roberto tried
to control his temper.

At first, the Pirates
weren't a very good team.
But they got better.
In 1960, they made it
to the World Series.

Roberto Clemente congratulates teammate Hal Smith (right) after Smith hit a three-run homer to help win the 1960 World Series for the Pittsburgh Pirates.

They played seven games
with the New York Yankees.
Roberto got a hit
in every game, and
the Pirates won the series.

The other Pirates had a party.
But Roberto went back out
to the field and hugged
his friends—the fans.

Roberto and Vera Cristina Zabala on their wedding day

Roberto spent his winters
at home in Puerto Rico.
There he met Vera Zabala.
In 1963, they got married
and built their own home.
They had three little boys.

The Clemente family at the ballpark for Roberto Clemente Night (above).
Roberto and Vera outside their home in Puerto Rico (below)

Roberto with his son Enrique
(Rickie) at the ballpark
(above) and at home (top right).
Roberto was awarded a new
sports car for his World
Series performance in 1971
(bottom right).

Life was good now
for Roberto Clemente.
It would get even better.

Chapter 4

A Leader

In 1966, Roberto batted .317.
He hit 29 home runs,
31 doubles, and 11 triples.

Sportswriters voted him
Most Valuable Player
of the year, and other
players voted him
Outstanding Player.

These 1966 Pirates all batted above .300: (left to right)
Matty Alou, Manny Mota, Roberto Clemente, and Willie Stargell.

In 1967, he batted .357.
Baseball's general managers
chose him as
"the best player today."

"He's not only the best today,"
said one manager.
"He's one of the best that's
ever played baseball."

July 24, 1970, was
"Roberto Clemente Night"
in Pittsburgh.
People came all the way
from Puerto Rico to honor him.

Roberto Clemente with Pirates manager Danny Murtagh

That night, someone
gave Roberto $6,000.
He gave the money to
Children's Hospital in Pittsburgh.

In 1971, the Pirates made it
to the World Series again.
This time they played
seven games with the
Baltimore Orioles.

Clemente was the leading hitter in the 1971
World Series. Clemente joins in
the locker-room celebration with
teammate Steve Blass (above)
after the Pirates won the series.

Clemente rounding third base after his fourth-inning
homer in the seventh game of the 1971 World Series

Once again, Roberto got
a hit in every game.
Once again, the Pirates
won the series.
This time, Roberto was
Most Valuable Player.

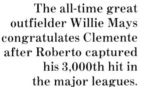

The all-time great outfielder Willie Mays congratulates Clemente after Roberto captured his 3,000th hit in the major leagues.

On September 30, 1972,
another great thing happened.
Roberto made hit number 3,000.
Only ten other men in the
major leagues had done that.

Chapter 5

More Than a Good Man

When Roberto was a boy,
he thought a lot
about baseball.
Now he was a great player,
and he thought a lot
about other people.

**Roberto Clemente
always had time
for his fans.**

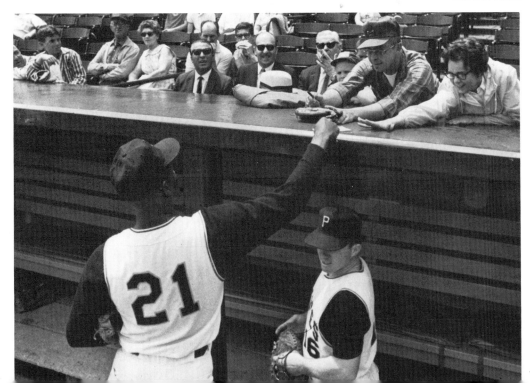

Clemente signing autographs for his fans (opposite).
Clemente was honored by the Baseball Writers Association
of America at a dinner in January 1972 (above).

He gave away money
to help people.
He visited sick children.

Athletic Court Jogging Area		Boxing	
Equestrian Center		Marina and Aquatic Center	
Volleyball Court		Olympic Swimming Pool	
Soccer Field		Tennis Court	
Amphitheater Gymnastics, Judo, and Wrestling		Archery Field	
Golf Course		Horse Barn	
Baseball Diamond		Camping Area	
Basketball Court		Commercial Shops	
Monument to Children and Sports		Bicycle Path	
Roberto Clemente Museum		Hotel	
Paid Announcements		Reflection Lake Drive	
Cafeteria		Go-Karts, Games	
Health Service		Dormitories	
Chapel		Administrative Offices	
Parking			

The plan for Roberto Clemente's Sports City in San Juan,
Puerto Rico (opposite page). The pictures in the key above match
those on the plan to show where each sport would be played.

He wanted to build a big
sports center in Puerto Rico
so children there could
learn to play different games.

AVE. ITURREGUI

Futuro
Expreso
Las Américas

Earthquake damage in Managua, the capital city of Nicaragua

On December 22, 1972,
a strong earthquake hit
the country of Nicaragua
in Central America.
Thousands of people died.
Many more needed help.

The earthquake destroyed many buildings and
left thousands homeless in Managua, Nicaragua

Roberto decided to collect
supplies in Puerto Rico
and take them to Nicaragua.

On New Year's Eve,
he got onto an old plane
with some other people
and the supplies.
The plane took off.

A few minutes later,
it crashed into the sea.
Everyone on board died,
including Roberto Clemente.

A diver examines the wreckage of the plane that crashed in
the sea, killing Roberto Clemente and four other people.

Vera Clemente and her sons (Enrique, Roberto, and Enrico) attended
a service in San Juan, Puerto Rico, in memory of Roberto in January.
Roberto Clemente's number was retired and his mother
Luisa (below, at left) and his wife Vera received his Pirate's uniform at
a ceremony in Pittsburgh, Pennsylvania, in 1973.

The Clemente family stands in front of the statue honoring Roberto Clemente at the Sports City in San Juan, Puerto Rico.

Roberto's father had wanted
him to be a good man.
When Roberto died,
he was more than that.
He was a great man.

Three months after his death,
the baseball writers voted
Roberto Clemente into the
National Baseball Hall of Fame.
He belonged there.

ROBERTO WALKER CLEMENTE
PITTSBURGH N. L. 1955-1972
MEMBER OF EXCLUSIVE 3,000-HIT CLUB. LED
NATIONAL LEAGUE IN BATTING FOUR TIMES.
HAD FOUR SEASONS WITH 200 OR MORE HITS
WHILE POSTING LIFETIME .317 AVERAGE AND
240 HOME RUNS. WON MOST VALUABLE PLAYER
AWARD 1966. RIFLE-ARMED DEFENSIVE STAR
SET N. L. MARK BY PACING OUTFIELDERS IN
ASSISTS FIVE YEARS. BATTED .362 IN TWO
WORLD SERIES, HITTING IN ALL 14 GAMES.

Clemente heads for
first base after
getting his 3,000th
hit on September 30,
1972. Roberto signs
autographs for two
young fans (below)
at the New York
World's Fair in 1964.

Roberto Clemente—Baseball Statistics

Lifetime batting average: .317
Four National League batting titles
Twelve Golden Glove awards for fielding
Three thousand hits
Played on 12 National League All-Star teams

Important Dates

1934   August 18—Born in Carolina, Puerto Rico, to Melchor and Luisa Clemente

1953   Began to play with Santurce Crabbers

1954   Went to Brooklyn Dodgers farm club in Montreal, Canada

1955   Signed with Pittsburgh Pirates

1963   Married Vera Zabala

1966   Voted Most Valuable Player of the year

1970   July 24—"Roberto Clemente Night" at Three Rivers Stadium, Pittsburgh

1971   Voted Most Valuable Player of World Series

1972   September 30—Made 3,000th hit

December 31—Died in plane crash off the coast of Puerto Rico

1973   Voted into National Baseball Hall of Fame

INDEX

Page numbers in boldface type indicate illustrations.

PHOTO CREDITS

ABOUT THE AUTHOR

Carol Greene has degrees in English literature and musicology. She has worked in international exchange programs, as an editor, and as a teacher of writing. She now lives in Webster Groves, Missouri, and writes full-time. She has published more than 100 books, including those in the Rookie Biographies series.